Clothes in Cold Weather

Miriam Moss

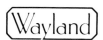

Costumes and Clothes

Children's Clothes
Clothes in Cold Weather
Clothes in Hot Weather
Fashionable Clothes
Hair and Make-up
How Clothes Are Made
National Costume
Sports Clothes
Theatrical Costume
Uniforms
Working Clothes

First published in 1988 by Wayland (Publishers) Ltd
61 Western Road, Hove, East Sussex BN3 1JD.

Editor: Deborah Elliott
Designer: Joyce Chester
Cover: Children in Baffin Island wearing warm fur coats and trousers.

British Library Cataloguing in Publication Data
Moss, Miriam
Clothes in cold weather — (costumes and clothes).
1. Clothing and dress — Cold weather conditions — Juvenile literature I. Title II.
Series
646' .3'0911 GT518

ISBN 1-85210-103-2

Photosetting by Direct Image Photosetting, Burgess Hill, West Sussex

Printed in Italy by G. Canale & C.S.p.A., Turin
Bound in France by A.G.M.

Some words in this book are
printed in **bold.** Their meanings
are explained in the glossary on
page 30.

Contents

What is Cold Weather?

When we think of cold weather we think of snow, frost, sleet and blizzards. In these weather conditions it can be dangerous not to wear warm, protective clothes. Even in less harsh cold weather it is important to wrap up well to avoid winter illnesses like colds and the flu.

The further you travel from the **Equator** the cooler it becomes, so the weather at the North and South **Poles** is extremely cold. In the **temperate** zones, the regions between the tropics and the Poles, the winters are less harsh. Sometimes freezing air currents, moving south from the North Pole and northwards from the Antarctic, can give very cold winters even in these temperate zones, (see pages 6-7). Cold winters cause the temperature of the air to drop dramatically. This is called the wind chill factor.

The higher the altitude (the height above sea level), the colder the air becomes. This is why

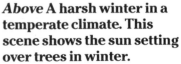

Above **A harsh winter in a temperate climate. This scene shows the sun setting over trees in winter.**

Left **Winters in most temperate areas are cold and usually wet. The most important clothing for people living in these regions are raincoats and umbrellas.**

snow falls on the mountainous regions of the world such as the Alps in Europe, the Rockies in North America, the Southern Alps of New Zealand, and even on mountains lying on the Equator.

When the temperature falls to 0°C water freezes. During a frost, much plant and animal life comes to a standstill because nearly every living thing contains water. Warm-blooded creatures, however, can survive in cold weather conditions because they are protected by their thick fur or blubber. We will see how humans, who are also warm blooded, manage to protect themselves from the cold.

Above **These German children's clothes are a mixture of natural and synthetic fibres.**

This Russian scientist working in the Arctic is kept warm by his fur-lined coat. The polar bear is protected by his thick fur.

Cold Lands

Different parts of the world receive different amounts of sunlight. The tropical regions each side of the Equator receive more direct sunlight because they are closer to the sun. Most people who have lived all their lives in the tropics have never seen ice or snow. The sunlight which reaches the North and South Poles has further to travel through the atmosphere and so is much weaker. This is why it is so cold at the North and South Poles.

Below **In temperate climates, the most suitable cold weather clothes are scarves, anoraks, overcoats, hats, gloves and boots.**

From the map we can see the different climates experienced all over the world. The illustrations are examples of the many different types of clothing worn in particular regions.

Arctic

Canada

South America

Antarctic

Polar region
Temperate region
Tropical region

The Arctic, the area around the North Pole, is a floating mass of ice, stretching from Siberia to Greenland and Alaska. The Antarctic is the region around the South Pole. It is a **continent,** made of rock and covered with ice which is sometimes 4,000m thick. The long winters in the Arctic and Antarctic are seasons of continuous frost and darkness. The summers are short although at midsummer the sun gives light for twenty-four hours each day; this is called the midnight sun.

Countries which experience temperate weather, such as Canada, South America, New Zealand, Japan, Scandinavia, Central and Eastern Europe and Britain have warm summers and cool or cold winters. The winters are usually much less harsh than in the polar regions, though sometimes temperatures can drop to below freezing. People have to dress up warmly in thick sweaters, scarves, boots, gloves and heavy overcoats. Often, it is difficult to get to work or school as snow has blocked the roads. Sometimes temperatures can drop so low that water pipes freeze and burst causing flooding. This can often mean a day off work or school.

Scandinavia

Britain

Central Europe

Eastern Europe

Japan

New Zealand

Antarctic

Protective Clothes

Clothes are extremely important in cold weather conditions. People who do not wear adequate clothing can sometimes die. In freezing conditions, a person can suffer from frostbite if their hands and feet are not properly protected. This occurs when the fluids in the body freeze and become ice crystals. The crystals prevent oxygen from reaching the blood cells and this causes **gangrene** in fingers and toes. In more severe cases, other parts of the body can also be affected by frostbite.

Cold weather is also the cause of another dangerous condition — **hypothermia.** This occurs when there is a rapid loss of body heat which cools the body to a dangerously low level. Sufferers can actually die because they are so cold. Clothes are also an important part of protection against sunburn in snowy conditions. The **ultraviolet** rays which cause sunburn, are reflected off the snow and are particularly strong in the thin air found at high altitudes. Protective goggles are often worn to avoid snow-blindness caused by the glare of the snow.

Different kinds of clothes are needed for different types of cold weather. When it is very cold and wet, waterproof clothes keep us warm and dry. In cold, wintry conditions we wear thick, wool pullovers and heavy cardigans. When going outside we need warm overcoats, woolly scarves, hats and gloves and boots to keep in our body heat. In bitterly cold, windy weather windproof clothes like anoraks and windcheaters stop the cold wind from penetrating and cooling down the air around

These children from Siberia in Russia are wearing warm hats with protective ear-flaps.

our bodies. In very extreme cold weather regions, such as Alaska, Greenland and Siberia, people wear clothes that have been specially adapted to suit the cold conditions. We shall see how the **Inuit**, Lapps and people who live high up in cold mountains have found suitable clothing to overcome the hostile weather conditions in which they live.

Baffin Island, off the northern coast of Canada, experiences freezing cold weather, so it is important that people dress up warmly in thick coats, boots and gloves.

Material Protection

In the past, people adapted to life in hostile weather conditions by using the skins of warm-blooded animals as protective clothing. The wool from sheep is very effective at keeping in body heat. **Unrefined** wool, which has not been treated with chemicals, is slightly oily and so has waterproof qualities. **Synthetic** waterproof materials used today are also very efficient.

Woven fabrics are treated with special water-resistant chemicals. The rain runs off the fabric and does not penetrate the fibres. Plastic is probably the most waterproof material.

Before today's synthetic materials like nylon were invented, people had to wear several layers of heavy clothing to keep warm. Now **cagoules**, for example, are made out of nylon coated with polyurethane — a lightweight, synthetic material which is very good at preventing body heat from escaping and keeping out the cold wind. Another way of keeping in body heat is to wear **thermal** underwear. This is made of a special material which can trap much of the body's heat. Some manufacturers have also been experimenting with metal reflective thread. This can reflect body heat back on to the body and so keep it warm in cold weather.

The parkas worn by these Inuit boys in Alaska, USA, are made from warm, well-insulated materials and are lined with fur.

Although it is essential to keep warm and dry in cold weather, comfort is also important. Clothes which are suitable for wearing in very cold conditions are made from materials which allow air to pass in and out. Sweat cools the body down, so clothes that allow moisture, like sweat, to build up are dangerous. In very cold conditions, sweat that is trapped in clothes will freeze, and this can be quite dangerous.

Countries which have a temperate climate have warm summers and cold winters. Woollen hats, waterproof boots and warm, waterproof suits are obviously the most effective winter clothing for these children from Sapporo in Japan.

Gloves, footwear and headgear

Gloves are an important form of protection against frostbite. They allow the heat which is given off by the body to circulate, but not escape. Gloves are made out of lots of different materials. People who work in freezing conditions sometimes wear silk gloves to prevent their hands from sticking to metal equipment. **Chamois** leather gloves are also often worn. In extremely cold weather, it is necessary to wear wool, **pile fibre** or felt mittens. On top of these, a pair of fur-lined leather gloves can be worn, or a pair of gloves made from a synthetic, waterproof material.

There are many different kinds of shoes and boots that people wear in cold and wet weather, from snow shoes to thigh-length waders. Rubber or plastic wellington boots are the most waterproof. Thick, army-type, leather boots with rubber soles are hard-wearing and very efficient in slippery conditions.

Above **Lapland is an area north of the Arctic Circle which has long, cold and severe winters. This Lapp is skilled in making these beautiful, reindeerskin boots which keep the feet warm in cold weather.**

This family from Winnipeg in Canada have wrapped up warmly in scarves, hats, gloves and boots, as protection against the bitterly cold weather.

Winters are very harsh in Minnesota, USA. Balaclavas are popular and efficient although they can look very sinister.

Fashionable, leather boots are warm but are not always waterproof. Sometimes they have to be treated with a special polish to prevent them from staining in the snow and rain.

Plastic mountaineering boots are tough, safe and waterproof but for extremely cold, dry weather *mukluks*, first worn by the Inuit (see pages 14-15), are popular. These are boots with rubber soles and a canvas upper lacing right up to the knee. They have a thick, felt inner boot and are worn with socks made from a blanket material. Hunting boots are also worn. These are very waterproof and warm but not suitable for wearing on ice. They have a thick, felt insole and inner boot. The rest of the boot is rubber with a waterproof upper and a high, leather cuff, laced up over the ankle.

Sock materials range from thin cotton to Norwegian rag wool which is oily and slightly waterproof. In cold weather it is best to wear lots of pairs of thick socks, as warm air is trapped between each pair. This allows moisture out but keeps warmth in.

There is a wide range of headgear worn in cold weather, from trackers' hats with flaps over the ears to **balaclavas**, made from wool and synthetic fleece materials. Woollen hats of every colour, with or without pompoms, are worn by people all over the world. About 30% of our body heat escapes from our head so wearing a hat is important in cold weather. Many people also wear earmuffs to keep their ears warm. These are pieces of fur worn over each ear and connected by a piece of plastic.

The Arctic and Antarctic

The Inuit

Many different groups of Inuit live in the Arctic. The Inuit adapted to the harsh, freezing environment in which they lived by building houses made of tightly packed snow which are sometimes called igloos. They also used teams of dogs to haul their possessions on wooden sleds called *komatics*.

Today, most Inuit live in permanent wooden houses and the dog teams have given way to motorized sleds, called skidoos. Inuit hunters and trappers use high-frequency radios to keep in touch as they travel long distances across the snow. Traditional Inuit clothes are woollen shirts and trousers under a loose-fitting jacket called a parka. The parka is lined with fur and fits snugly round the head, neck and hips. Their tall boots are made of **caribou** skin and are called *kamiks*.

These Canadian Inuit children are wearing clothes made from caribou skin. Their outfits are warm but bulky.

Above Inuit hunters travel across the snow on skidoos, which are motorized sledges.

Most Inuit today wear a mixture of traditional and modern dress. They wear jeans, shirts and sweaters. In winter these are worn with nylon or handmade parkas. The light, cotton parkas worn in milder weather are called *kuspaks*.

The Inuit boots are called *mukluks* and are made of sealskin, caribou or muskox fur and usually have moosehide or sealskin soles. The Inuit wear sealskin mittens which come up over their sleeves to keep out the cold and are often trimmed with wolf, fox or bear fur. Some hunters wear parkas made of white canvas to **camouflage** themselves from the animals in the snowy landscape. They also wear warm underwear made of material filled with soft, **down** feathers.

Notice the different kinds of clothes worn by these Inuit. All are designed to protect the wearer against the cold.

The Lapps

Lapland is the name of an area of Scandinavia and the USSR where the reindeer-herding Lapps live. Winters in Lapland are long, cold and severe, with snow lying on the ground for seven months of the year.

The Lapps used to herd reindeer and build temporary homes from branches and skins as they moved from place to place. Today, most Lapps have well-equipped homes with televisions, and drive cars and snow scooters. Lapp schoolchildren wear anoraks and jeans and use digital watches whereas their parents could tell the time from the position of the sun. Many Lapps today wear a mixture of traditional and modern dress. Traditional Lapp costumes are brightly coloured and beautifully decorated. Lapp women used to weave material by hand on looms. The tunic is called a *kolte*. It is made of a deep blue felt with bands of red, yellow and green. The trousers are narrow at the calf and are also made of felt.

Above Hats worn by Swedish Lapps are only used on special occasions.

This Lapp reindeer herder wears warm, traditional clothes and a shawl at work.

These are changed in winter for reindeerskin leggings which give extra warmth. Thick gloves and reindeerskin coats are also worn in freezing weather.

The women wear bonnets with flaps to protect their ears from the cold. Lapp men in Norway and Finland wear large floppy hats with four points which are known as 'hats of the four winds'. In Sweden the Lapp men wear hats with a large red pompom on top whereas in Russia the Lapp men wear square caps with a fur-trimmed border.

These Lapp children, playing on the lake shore, are wearing traditional *koltes* and hats with warm mittens and wellington boots.

Moccasins, made from pieces of reindeerskin sewn together, are traditional Lapp footwear. Instead of socks, dry grass is often stuffed into the shoe to make it a snug fit. The grass is dried out at night ready to be worn the next day.

Polar explorers and scientist

The first Polar explorers wore thick furs and snowshoes. Today's Polar scientists and explorers wear a combination of different layers of clothes depending on the weather conditions and the kind of activities being undertaken. This way of dressing is called the 'layer principle' and is an efficient way of surviving in bitterly cold weather.

The inner layer is called the 'vapour transmission layer' and is made up of thermal **long johns** and a long-sleeved vest made of a synthetic material, often Meraklon. This material is chosen because it is easy to wash and dry. It is also hardwearing and takes the moisture away from the body. Each person, however, has their own particular preference and some prefer to wear flannel pyjamas as underwear!

The next layer is called the '**insulation layer**' and consists of a shirt made of a synthetic or wool mixture. A heavy, Norwegian wool sweater is worn on top. Trousers are made of heavy moleskin or **cavalry twill** which are warm and windproof materials. If it is extremely cold a pile fibre, zipped sweater and trousers, or down duvet suit, is added. The pile fibre is hardwearing, light, warm, and easy to dry out.

The outer layer is the protective layer and is made from a closely woven, natural cotton material like fine canvas. Windproof trousers and a full-length, hooded anorak with drawstrings at the waist and ankles are comfortable to wear.

Freezing winds in the Antarctic can be very dangerous if you are not suitably protected. This scientist is wearing an extremely warm, well-insulated outfit and goggles which protect his eyes.

Above Scientists working in the Antarctic have to wear several layers of warm clothing.

Explorers still sometimes cross vast snowy plains on sledges pulled by teams of huskies.

Mountain People

Mountain weather

The weather in mountainous regions varies with the height of the mountains. The higher the altitude the thinner the air is, and the lower the air pressure. This causes the temperature to drop because there is less air than at sea level to hold the heat reflected from the land. The temperature falls by about 1°C for every 150m gained in height. This means that high mountains, even on the Equator, are always capped by snow and ice. The snow line on a mountain is the line above which there is always snow. This is at about 5,000m near the Equator, at about 2,750m in the Alps and at sea level in Antarctica.

Mountains are some of the wettest and windiest places in the world. The world's highest wind speed of 371 kph was recorded on Mount Washington in New Hampshire, USA. The cold air in the mountains rolls downhill and collects in hollows. These are called frost hollows and are very cold indeed at night. The sun's rays, however, are very powerful at high altitudes and it is very easy to become sunburnt even though the temperature is low. The clothes worn by people living high up in the mountains not only have to protect them from the cold, wind and rain but from the sun's powerful rays. Most people who live in the mountains are farmers. Because they have to herd animals across icy torrents and glaciers looking for pasture land, they need tough, warm clothes.

Most mountain people, like those living in the Norwegian mountains, live in sheltered

These women live high up in the cold Himalayan mountains, between India and Tibet.

valleys or on level ground between mountain ranges. Visitors to mountainous regions may suffer from **mountain sickness** because they are not used to the thinner air. People who live at high altitude, are not affected as they have bigger lungs which take in more air, and larger hearts with which to pump the increased number of blood cells carrying oxygen around the body.

Life can be very harsh for people who have to live and work in cold, mountainous regions.

The Indians of the Andes

The Andes Mountains of South America stretch from the Caribbean to Cape Horn. The Indians live in the mountain valleys where the temperature can drop to well below freezing at night.

Indian women spin and weave **llama** wool into clothes and blankets. Like sheep's wool, it is very efficient at keeping people warm. Of all the people living in the Andes, the Aymara women are the most colourfully dressed. They wear skirts, or *polleras*, made of brilliantly-coloured, heavy cotton gathered in tightly at the waist. Several of these skirts are worn at the same time. The number of skirts a woman wears is a sign of how rich she is. A blouse of rough cotton is worn over the *pollera*. A woollen blanket is doubled over the shoulders for warmth. Women also wear brightly

In Cuenca in Ecuador, as in many other parts of the world, people dress according to the weather.

Above This Quechua woman wears a hat to shield her eyes from the winter sun and woollen clothes to keep warm.

Above This Quechua woman from the mountainous Cuzco region of Peru is carrying her daughter in a brightly-coloured *aguayo*.

striped, cotton shawls, called *aguayos* in which a baby is often carried. The men wear rough, baggy cotton trousers, covered by a long, earth-coloured poncho and a warm, knitted hat called a *chullo*.

The Otavalo people of Ecuador farm in the high mountain valleys. The men can be recognized by their long, dark blue ponchos, worn over white trousers. They wrap their ponchos around themselves to keep out the cold mountain air and keep their heads warm by wearing wide-brimmed, felt hats.

The more wealthy families have mechanized looms. Some weave using synthetic fibres like orlon which saves time previously spent washing, dyeing and spinning the wool. They make warm, brightly-coloured ponchos, blankets and shawls.

The beautifully designed fabrics made by the Otavalo people are sold all over the world.

Himalayan peoples

The Himalayan Mountains, and other neighbouring mountain ranges, contain some of the world's highest mountains. This includes Mount Everest which is 8,848m high. These mountains contain huge expanses of snow and great freezing glaciers which feed several rivers that help to **irrigate** land in India and Pakistan.

Left These young boys who live in the Himalayas are dressed in woollen clothes.

Below This woman is milking a yak. She is wearing a goatskin over her back as protection against the biting wind.

How many different kinds of cold weather clothes can you see in this street scene of Ladakh, Tibet?

The weather in these mountains is different in summer and winter and can be very changeable at all times. Winters in the mountains are very harsh. The town of Leh in Ladakh is cut off from the rest of India for six months of the year because the snow makes the only road impassable. Like Tibetans, Ladakhis who live on the Tibetan Plateau more than 3,000m above sea level, wear thick clothes made out of sheep or **yak** skins to protect them from the cold.

The women of Ladakh wear their coats, which are slung over their shoulders from a cord, with the fur on the inside. For them it is more important to keep warm than to show off the fur.

Shepherds in the foothills of the Himalayas wear a *gaddi* jacket. This is a thick, rough tweed jacket made from unrefined wool and is made-to-measure by the village tailor.

Working Clothes

Working clothes worn in cold weather vary enormously depending on the work conditions. It is dangerous to be either too hot or too cold at work as it can lead to a loss of concentration and so to accidents. Because it is also important that workers are mobile as well as warm, the layers of warm clothes must not hamper their movements.

In extreme conditions special clothes must be worn. Divers in the freezing waters of the North Sea need special protection while inspecting or repairing underwater oil rig equipment. They wear waterproof wet suits made of rubber. These let in only a thin layer of water which the body heat warms up. Icelandic fishermen wear thick sweaters, watertight oilskins, tough, warm protective

Canadian fur trappers wear warm anoraks and hats. Many people feel strongly against killing animals in order to sell their skins.

gloves and thigh-length boots to save them from the lashing rain and the icy sleet.

Astronauts working in space, where it is extremely cold, wear space suits which cover them completely with many layers for warmth. The first layer is an all-in-one knitted suit. The other layers keep their body heat at an even temperature and insulate them against the harsh cold.

This photographer is taking pictures in the Canadian Arctic. Because he has to use his hands when taking photographs, he wears gloves that not only keep him warm but also allow plenty of freedom of movement.

Below **Divers are properly insulated against extreme cold weather conditions, in their rubber wet suits.**

Winter Sports Clothes

Wearing the right clothes when taking exercise is very important because the body heats up and must not cool down too quickly. Ice hockey players, for example, 'warm up' wearing warm outer clothes to avoid muscle strain. Skaters sometimes practise on the ice in quilted, waterproof anoraks filled with light, warm padding. It is particularly important for sports clothes to **ventilate** the body and stop moisture from collecting. Children brought up in places like Canada or Norway learn to ski at an early age. They wear tracksuits with warm, brushed-cotton linings that insulate and ventilate the body. In cold weather, all over the world, children love to go ice skating, snowballing and sledging.

The sport of riding snow buggies is becoming more and more popular in cold weather. This rider is practising in Minnesota, USA.

Mountaineers need strong, spiked boots and warm, waterproof clothing. Skiers wear thermal underwear with tough salopettes, which are stretchy trousers or dungarees with a high back. Down waistcoats called body warmers are often worn on top of thick polo-neck jumpers. In very cold weather, windproof jackets are also worn. Like ice speed skaters, Olympic downhill racing skiers need light, warm, tight-fitting clothes for speed. They wear a special synthetic material that only allows a little air through it.

There are all sorts of specialized clothes which have been adapted for different sports. You can see that it is important to wear suitably warm clothes when taking exercise in cold weather — even if you are just going outside for a snowball fight.

Right The special clothes worn by people taking part in energetic sports in cold weather, are not only warm and protective but also allow for plenty of freedom of movement.

Left Skiing is a popular sport in cold weather conditions in many countries. This family are exercising on Blue Mountain in Canada.

Glossary

Balaclavas Close-fitting, woollen hoods that cover the ears and most of the head. Named after a place in the Crimea, where they were first worn during the Crimean War (1854-56).

Cagoules Lightweight anoraks which usually come down to the knees.

Camouflage To disguise something by making it the same colour as the surroundings so it will blend in.

Caribou A large North American reindeer.

Cavalry twill A strong, woollen fabric used to make trousers.

Chamois A soft, yellowish leather material, originally made from the skin of the chamois goat.

Continent One of the divisions of the world's land surface. The five continents are: Europe, Africa, Asia, North and South America and Australia.

Down Soft and fluffy bird feathers.

Equator An imaginary line making a circle around the earth, halfway between the North and South Poles.

Gangrene The rotting of flesh, usually caused by the blood supply being cut off.

Hypothermia An extremely low body temperature usually suffered by old people who are exposed to very cold weather.

Insulation layer A layer of clothing which keeps heat in and stops cold from reaching the body.

Inuit People from Arctic North America and Greenland.

Irrigate To water land by means of canals or water pipes.

Llama A South American animal whose woollen coat is made into warm clothes.

Long johns Warm underpants with long legs.

Mountain sickness An illness suffered by some people when they go up to high altitudes.

Pile fibre A strong, soft, warm material.

Poles The north and south ends of the world.

Synthetic A material made by mixing certain chemicals together.

Temperate Weather which is moderate and not extreme. The temperate areas of the world lie between the tropics and the polar regions.

Thermal Something that gives off heat and warmth.

Ultraviolet rays Rays from the sun that are stronger at higher altitudes.

Unrefined Substances which have not been treated with chemicals.

Ventilate To allow fresh air to pass in and out.

Yak A Tibetan ox. Its thick coat can be used to make warm clothes.

Books to read

Eskimos — The Inuit of the Arctic by J. H. Greg Smith (Wayland Publishers Ltd, 1984)

Explorers by Tim Healey (Macdonald Educational, 1980)

Indians of the Andes by Marion Morrison (Wayland Publishers Ltd, 1985)

Just Look at Clothes by Brenda Ralph Lewis (Macdonald Educational, 1986)

Lapps, Reindeer Herders of Lapland by Alan James (Wayland Publishers Ltd, 1986)

Let's go to Canada by Keith Lye (Franklin Watts 1983)

Living with the Eskimos by Bernard Plance (Moonlight Publishing Ltd, 1986)

Mountains by Keith Lye (Wayland Publishers Ltd, 1986)

Mountains by Roy Woodcock (Macdonald Educational, 1980)

Polar Regions by David Lambert (Wayland Publishers Ltd, 1987)

The Soviet Union by James Riordan (Macdonald Educational, 1975)

We Live in the Asian USSR by E. Ryakbo (Wayland Publishers Ltd, 1984)

We Live in Canada by Jack Brickenden (Wayland Publishers Ltd, 1984)

We Live in Chile by Alex Huber (Wayland Publishers Ltd, 1985)

We Live in the European USSR by E. Ryakbo (Wayland Publishers Ltd, 1984)

We Live in Sweden by Stephen Keeler and Chris Fairclough (Wayland Publishers Ltd, 1984)

Index

Acknowledgements
The publisher would like to thank the following for providing the pictures used to illustrate this book:

Bryan and Cherry Alexander 7 (top), 8, 9, 12 (top), 13, 14, 15, 16 (bottom), 17, 21, 22 (bottom), 24 (bottom) 25, 27, 28; Chris Gibb 24 (top); Marion and Tony Morrison 22 (top), 23 (top); Picturepoint 4 (bottom), 11, 18 19 (top), 20; Malcolm S. Walker 6-7 (map); Wayland Picture Library 5 (bottom), 16 (top), 26, 29 (bottom); Zefa 4 (top), 5 (top), 10, 12 (bottom), 19 (bottom), 29 (top).